HOW MANY POINTS FOR A PANDA?

Written and illustrated by
HILDA OFFEN

For Hannah and Libby Fairless

Published by TROIKA
First published 2019
1 3 5 7 9 10 8 6 4 2
Text and illustrations copyright © Hilda Offen 2019
The moral rights of the author/ illustrator have been asserted
All rights reserved
A CIP catalogue record for this book is available from the British Library
ISBN 978-1-912745-11-1
Printed in Poland

Troika Books Ltd
Well House, Green Lane, Ardleigh CO7 7PD, UK
www.troikabooks.com

Contents

Talking and Squawking

Here, There and Everywhere

Monsters and Magic

Monster Attack!

Marie is a monster;
She says "Come on, Doug!
Just give your sister
A nice little hug."

Then her face goes all green
As horns sprout from her head.
Her hands become claws
And her eyes turn bright red.

Why does she do it?
I haven't annoyed her.
I charge round the house,
Trying hard to avoid her.

But when Mum comes in
And says "Just let Doug be!"
Then the monster dissolves
And turns back to Marie.

Silvery Shoes

My friend Libby Lou has silvery shoes –
That's what I'd wear if they'd just let me choose.

She won't take them off – she wears them to school;
She's worn them for swimming three lengths of the pool.

As she cycles and skateboards, they sparkle and shine,
They flicker and glitter – I wish they were mine!

She wears them for climbing, kung-fu and gymnastics;
She wears them for football – her shooting's fantastic!

At night she's a firefly – she sparkles and glows
As she twists and she turns on her silvery toes.

I wish that my shoes were like yours, Libby Lou –
Then I'd sparkle and glitter and shine just like you.

The Buzzaboo

You should never say "Boo!" to a wild Buzzaboo –
He'd throw custard all over you, that's what he'd do.
He'd roar and he'd growl and run off with your shoes
And your socks and your hat. He's really bad news.

A Buzzaboo lives in our old garden shed;
His face is ferocious, his ears are brick red.
He sits in a nest made of shoes, hats and socks
And listens all day to his ten chiming clocks.

He's the size of a hippo; his fur is bright blue.
His nose is a trumpet; he howls "Hooty-hoo!"
I hear him at night when he's out on the prowl.
"Don't be silly!" says Mum. "It's only an owl."

Hooty-hoo!

But I know that he's there; you can see where he's been;
He rolls in the flowerbeds and chomps up the greens.
Buzzaboos are the limit! They're rough and they're bad;
If you meet one, just run – and keep running like mad!

Invisible

Two faces, red, like birds of prey,
Swoop down on me – please go away!
Their voices cackle, cluck and coo:
"What's **your** name, then? How old are you?"

I close my eyes and squeeze them tight;
I'm hidden now – I'm out of sight.
"Isn't she funny? Is she shy?"
"She's closed her eyes – I wonder why?"

I can't see them – they can't see me;
Their voices fade and I float free.
Now I'm alone, I hear instead
Only the thoughts inside my head.

And all I see is sun-shimmer,
Dazzle, sparkle, glint and glimmer.
Colours splinter, flake and flare
Into the golden arc of air.

I'm safe in here; I think I'll stay
Until the birds have flown away.

Sea Mist

The world is hushed and holds its breath;
There's no horizon now –
Only a wall of silver-grey,
A blankness, silent, still.
Nearer to where the shore should be
A little boat is floating in the air.
It hangs there, poised, about to sail.

The sea-mist thickens, rolls inland;
It strolls the front with muffled tread
And flows into the side-streets of the town.
Meanwhile, the boat has disappeared;
Catching the silver tide, it's slipped away –
Over the bandstand and the pier,
Into the reaches of the upper air.

Whale

What would you do
If a great blue whale
Tipped you into the sea
With a flick of his tail?

And what would you do
If he swallowed you whole,
Along with a haddock,
Some cod and a sole?

16

I'd tickle his tummy
With the end of my scarf;
I'd give him the hiccups –
Make him giggle and laugh;
And soon he'd be gasping
"Hic! Hic! No more!"
Then he'd hiccup me out
And I'd land on the shore.

Hic! Hic! Hic!

Hic!

Icarus

You've no idea how long it took
To build those wings – it made me ill.
The gathering of the feathers set me off –
I was sneezing, choking, all day long.
Through streaming eyes, I stirred the melted wax
And helped to glue our plumage to the frame.
Precision was the order of the day; it was
"That's out of line! Unpick it! Start again!"

I almost died of fright before the launch;
He led the way – called me to follow on.
And so I leaped; I shadowed him
Across the sea – a winged automaton.

He went on shouting orders : "Not too high!
Avoid the waves! Now steer a steady course!"
But suddenly a thrill ran through my body –
I'd never felt as free as this before.
I swooped and soared and swooped again –
Beat upwards to a feathered cloud, cut through
The dazzling crystals; knew myself re-born.
His voice grew fainter; soon it died away.

And then I burst into the blue
And headed for the sun.

The Dive

The water's clear, the water's cool;
I dive into the glassy pool
And swim down through the green half-light,
Past shoals of fish in liquid flight –
Where jewel-encrusted monsters haunt
The coral caves and mermaids flaunt
Their rainbow tails; where treasures lie
And turtles croon a lullaby.
Sea-horses neigh; a serpent curls
Around a casket filled with pearls ...

"Stop staring in that puddle, Dee!"
Calls Mum. "Come in – it's time for tea."

Secrets and Shadows

The Spell

"Castles! Candles! Cobwebs! Cats!"

She shouts to wake the echoes
That drowse inside the railway arch.
And high above her, in the inky dark,
The sleepers stir and answer back:

"Castles! Candles! Cobwebs! Cats!"

Just like a stone that skims the pond –
Each hop shorter than the one before –
The echoes fade, with every phrase
A little fainter than the last.

The stone drops down – but not the spell;
It travels on, through time and space
And echoes round amongst the stars:

"Castles! Candles! Cobwebs! Cats!
Castles! Candles! Cobwebs! Cats!
Castles! Candles! Cob .... "

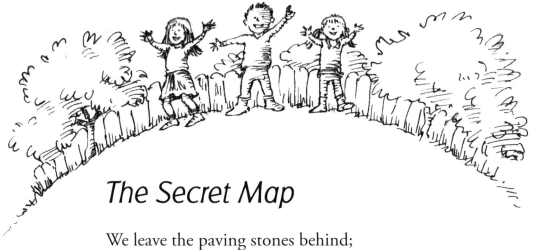

The Secret Map

We leave the paving stones behind;
Our feet have formed these narrow paths,
Exploring, treading, year by year.

We scramble up the hollowed track –
Steady ourselves along the ridge,
The goose-grass grasping at our legs,
While, far below, the grown-ups call,
"Be careful!" "Watch your step!"

But our steps made this criss-cross map –
These tiny tracks; they're ours alone.
Our noses know the smell of earth and leaves,
Our feet the dips and bumps and stones
That guide us upwards on the snaking trail
Until we reach the small trees by the fence.

We are the conquerors! The summit's ours!
Our secret world spreads out below.

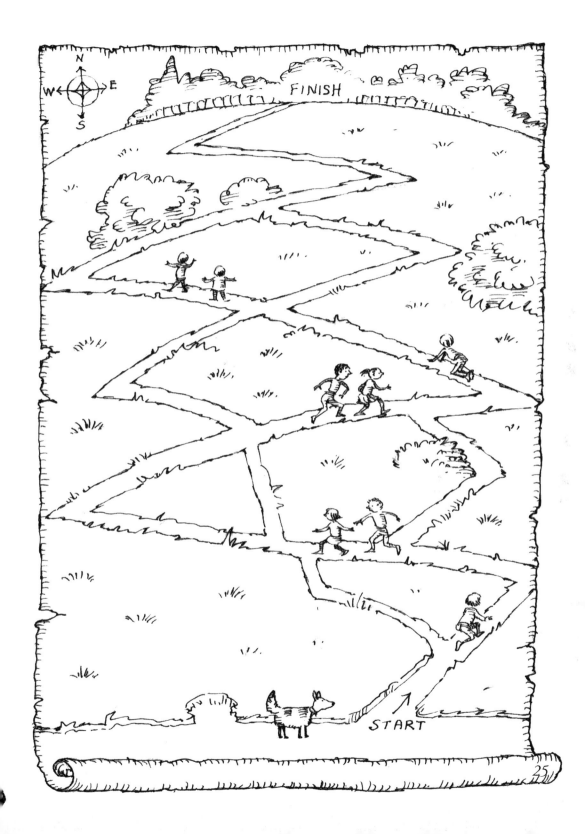

Shadows

How many shadows in the past
Have fallen on this wall?
Sharp electric light casts mine –
But was there once a time,
In the soft gas-light, long ago,
(When mantles flaked and fluttered
Like white moths) that someone
Just like me was framed upon this wall?
And with his hands made shadow-shapes –
A witch, a swan, a hare perhaps –
To make the young ones laugh?

And once, maybe, by candle-light,
An earlier such another watched in awe
As his giant shadow loomed upon the wall,
Shape-shifting into monstrous forms –
Then flickered, leaped and ebbed away
Into the corners of the room.

New Sister

We walked the bounds with you
And traced the limits of your small domain –
Showed you the bedrock of your world-to-be.
The Unknown Tree, the sequinned stream,
The wood-pile, mouse-runs, cyclamen –
We named them into life for you.

And later still, on Stanage Edge,
We sheltered in the curve of rock,
Made verses for you, silvered songs
To wish you on your way.

Crows curled upon the steel-eyed air
And far below, the world streamed out,
Encrypted, silent; waiting for you –
Waiting to be read.

Fossil Footprints

"Some forty thousand years ago, a group of humans walked along this river mouth and headed west; they left their footprints in the mud. A smaller set of prints trails after them; they indicate the presence of a child."

Are we there yet?
It's starting to get dark.
The others trudge ahead –
I can hear them grumbling,
Mumbling to each other.
We've gathered shellfish
From the rocks and now
We're off again –
I don't know why;
I don't know where.
I wish they'd stop and rest.
My feet are sinking in the mud;
It's hard to walk.

Down on the shore
White birds are settling.
The sky's turned red;
So has the sea.
Are we there yet?

The Bright Side

One day they noticed that the butterflies had gone.
"A shame!" they said. "They were such pretty things,
Fluttering around the place like that. But never mind!"

Quite soon the bees stopped droning through the flowers.
"Such nasty stings!" they said. "It's no great loss."

A morning came when all the birds fell quiet.
"Look on the bright side – now we'll get some sleep.
They kicked up such a racket, didn't they?" they said.

Next spring the trees were lifeless, brittle, bare.
"It's for the best!" they sighed. "Such nuisances,
Scattering their leaves about the street each year."

Soon after this, the flowers failed to bloom.
"Oh well!" they said. "Let's put some decking down."

And they went on looking on the bright side ....

Maureen Lee

You were my hero, Maureen Lee –
You, with your long black plaits
And your green, green eyes, just like a cat's;
I wanted to be like you.

I wanted to be as bold as you –
Face bullies; make the big boys laugh.
First into the skipping rope!
Winner of every racc on earth!
Superstar! Top of the tree!
I wanted to **be** you, Maureen Lee.

I made up stories in my head;
I saved you from an icy pond,
So we became best friends.
And we fought pirates, bandit hordes
And saw off highwaymen.
But how it happened – I don't know –
You always seemed to take the lead;
I trailed behind; I was too slow.

And then one day it dawned on me –
I'd never be you, Maureen Lee.
I said goodbye; I set you free.

I had to learn how to be me.

Old Glass

No-one knows what I see
Through my aunt's window-pane;
I can shatter the world –
Then build it all up again.

Bubbles and ripples,
Wave-marks and flaws;
The old glass is pitted
With scratches and scores.

With my eye to this tear-drop
I make everything alter –
Things see-saw and shudder;
They tremble and falter.

I look to the left
And the traffic-lights shake;
I can make people wobble –
They quiver and quake.

Now I lop off the top
Of that tall poplar tree;
It separates – hovers –
And then it floats free.

And no-one suspects
The power of my glance.
It's magic! I'm making
The church steeple dance.

Secret

I told a secret to my friend;
She told it to her brother.
He shared it with the boy next door –
He went and told his mother.

And so it sped around the town
And passed from street to street,
Until it travelled back to me –

34

Talking and Squawking

The Parrot

I hop upon my perch; I screech –
I'm getting ready for my speech.
A sea of faces waits below;
I puff my chest and squawk "Hallo!
What's your name, then? Hallo! Hallo!"

They speak at once: "My name is Ben."
"This is Marie." "And this is Glenn."
"This here is Alice." "I'm Elaine."
"I'm Jim!" "I'm Gemma!" "And I'm Wayne."

When there's a hush I click my beak.
I preen myself and start to speak.
I stretch my wings and say "Hallo!
What's your name, then? Hallo! Hallo!"

They take deep breaths and start again ...

The Tour

Now here we have the sixth Lord Vaughan,
Complete with ruff and hunting horn –
Don't touch the blinds, son, daylight spoils
The depth and brilliance of the oils.

(It's cold in here and rather dark;
I'd like to be out in the park.)

We're entering the Yellow Room,
Its hangings made on Belgian looms.
Look up! The dome is painted blue,
With summer clouds and small birds, too.

(Out there, the sun shines in the sky
And real clouds float and real birds fly.)

And now we reach the panelled hall,
With antlers covering each wall.
Observe the pheasants, flowers and ribbons
Carved by the famous Grinling Gibbons!

(There's deer out by the waterfall;
Real poppies sway and pheasants call.)

You see that gold and silver chair?
King Charles the Second once sat there.
Where are you going? Not that door!
We're only half-way through the tour!

(That's it! I'm off! I've had enough
Of kings and carvings – all that stuff.
It's better out here in the sun –
Now all I want to do is run!)

39

Remembering

Look at this photo.
I'm holding a duckling;
I'd almost forgotten till now –
The smell of the hay
And the small lambs bleating
Out on the brow of the hill.

And now I remember
The weight of its body –
Its soft, downy weight,
Like a light puff of air.
I can still feel its warmth
And its little heart beating
Against my cupped hands;
I can still feel it now.

Why?

Why do cats purr?
Why do dogs bark?
Why can't I play
Out in the park?
And why does Jay
Sing out of tune?
And why is there
A sun and moon?
Why do the stars
Stay in the sky?
Why is it birds
Know how to fly?
And why do snails
Leave silver trails?
Why are there sharks
And killer whales?

Why can't I have
More apple pie?
And why do babies
Scream and cry?
Why am I young
And Grandma's old?
And summer's hot
And winter's cold?
Why's water wet?
Why's paper dry?
And why does grandad
Wear that tie?
Why don't toffees
Grow on trees?
Why are there wasps
And buzzing bees?

Why must I go to bed at eight?
And why can Josh stay up so late?
Why do I have to go to school?
Why can't I swim across the pool?
And when I say it wasn't me
Who pushed Miranda off that tree
Why do you frown? And why, oh why,
Won't you accept my alibi?
Why does it rain? Why does it snow?
I want to know! I want to know!
Why do you purse your lips and sigh
When all I want to know is – **Why?**

The Dancing Tree

Each time the school puts on a play
I hope I'll be the star –
I've only been a five-barred gate
And Second Sheep so far.

I'd learned the part of Peter Pan –
I know I'd got it sussed.
So when they said I'd play a tree,
Imagine my disgust!

So there I stood, leaves on my head,
Pretending to be an oak,
When Peter Pan forgot his lines –
Time for my master-stroke!

I waved my arms and someone laughed;
I mimed a sudden breeze.
More laughter! So I did a dance
Around the other trees.

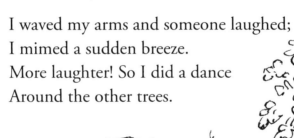

But then an arm shot from the wings
And hauled me from the stage
And there stood Mrs Oliver,
Her face bright red with rage.

She tapped me on my cardboard trunk,
Peered through my greenery
And snarled

You'll never act again –
That's it! You'll just do Scenery.

But someone's put a thing online
(Who wrote it I don't know).
"Top marks to the Dancing Tree –
The high spot of the show."

A Field

"Describe a field!" said Mrs Brown.
"Look carefully – then write it down."
I've found a field, I'm sitting in it –
I'll start the writing in a minute.

But what? What can I write?

Bees are buzzing, something squeaks,
Crickets chirp and grass-stems creak.
It's noisy here; I can't think straight –
I really need to concentrate.

What can I write?

Poppies tickle, daisies sway
In an irritating way.
Pollen's getting up my nose –
And Mrs Brown wants deathless prose?

Help!

Striped caterpillars creep around
And beetles scuttle on the ground.
Ugh! There's a spider in my ear –
I think it's time to disappear.

I've still got no ideas.

It's hopeless! What a pointless day!
It's just a field – what can I say?
The grass is green, the sky is blue?
I know! A unicorn or two –
And knights in shining armour, fighting!
Yes! That will make it more exciting!

That's what I'll write!

Greetings

"Why! Haven't you grown **tall**!" they say.
I smile and nod my head.
But secretly I think "That's strange –
What if I'd shrunk instead?"

"Why! Haven't you got **small**!" they'd cry
"Much smaller than last year!"
Mouse-sized, I'd smile and nod my head
And then I'd disappear.

Here, There and Everywhere

Bike-snatcher

Whilst riding one day by the shore
I encountered a young dinosaur.
He said "That's what I'd like!"
Helped himself to my bike
And cycled away with a roar.

49

My Family Tree

May I present my family tree?
The good-looking boy at the bottom is me.
Next up, on a branch, is Ella our cat
And Bertie the dog, who is wearing a hat.
Above them sits Dad – he's playing the flute
And holding Colette, in her kangaroo suit.
On a neighbouring branch is my mother, the star;
She's dancing and playing upon her guitar.
Look up at my grandads! They're keep-fit fanatics;
They seem to be doing a spot of gymnastics.
Nanny Barlow's up there, moulding pots out of clay
And Gran Potter is shooing some eagles away.

But as for my cousins, my uncles and aunties –
Sorry! This tree is full. We've run out of branches.

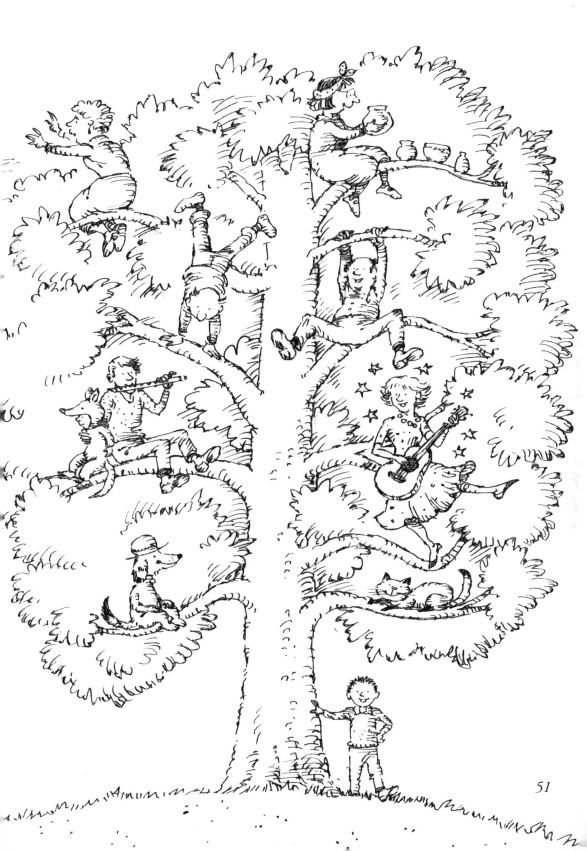

The Fortune-Teller

There once was an old fortune-teller
Who spent most of her time in a cellar.
When they asked "Will it snow?"
She snapped "I don't know!
Now – where did I put my umbrella?"

Gorilla

At the pet-shop my Auntie Priscilla
Was offered a lowland gorilla.
She said "He's too tall!
I want something small –
A cat or perhaps a chinchilla."

How Many Points for a Panda?

Two points for a rabbit – squirrels score four;
Badgers and foxes and weasels score more.
This is the game that we play on the train –
We play it over and over and over again.

"I've got ten points already!" said my sister Amanda.
Then a little voice piped "How many points for a panda?"
We all turned and stared and Amanda said "Where?
Whereabouts was this panda?" And Claire said "Back there!"
"I don't believe you!" said Mike. "Huh! What was it like?"
"Like a panda," said Claire. "It had just parked its bike
And climbed to the top of a very tall tree;
It was licking a lolly and scratching its knee –
And I think it was wearing a Mexican hat –
Now! How many points am I getting for that?"

"Full marks for invention!" said Mum. "What a brain!"
Then we came to our station and got off the train.

Baby Boots

Among the photos on the shelf
Are pictures of my baby self.
There's more of them upon the wall –
How is it that I've grown so tall?

My baby boots stand in the rain –
I'll never put them on again.
They're filled with earth and planted up
With pansies, pinks and buttercups.

My rocking horse lies in the shed.
I ride a bicycle instead.
And I wear trainers, run and swim
And do gymnastics at the gym.

But sometimes, when I take a break
And glimpse those photos on the shelf –
Oh! How I miss my baby boots!
And how I miss my baby self!

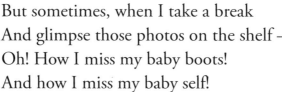

Here We Come!

Clear the pavements!
Sound the hooters!
Here we come –
We're on our scooters!

Parents chase us,
Puffing, blowing,
Shouting "Stop!
Watch where you're going!"

But we go faster –
We don't care.
We whizz along;
We're free as air.

So clear the paths
And sound the hooters!
We're off to school –
We're on our scooters!

Cranes

Sharp on the dot of nine
The cranes stir into life
Above the building site.
Like long-necked birds,
They curtsey, bow,
And start their stately dance.
They dip and turn and turn again –
White phantoms, elegant and spare,
Capped by their top-knots
Of red fire.

By nightfall, they have flown;
Only their scarlet crests remain –
A fiery constellation
Upon the western sky.

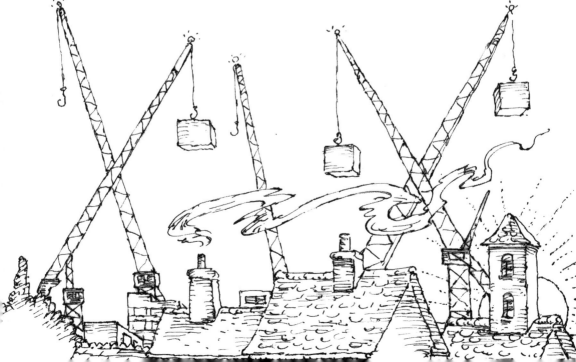

Midsummer

Midday in the park:
Mid-summer's day.
The acers stand, entranced –
Toy farmyard trees
Upon a shadowed base.
Dragonflies go flickering
From pond to pond
And somewhere overhead
A small plane drones.

The woods are washed
With indigo
And pink-tongued dogs
Lie panting in the shade.
A breeze begins to whisper,
Rises, falls,
Like a warm breath.
And all the while,
In the green depth
Of leaves,
Wood-pigeons croon.

59

The Naming of Clouds

Luke Howard classified clouds
In eighteen-hundred and two;
Gave them numbers, gave them names,
Names that grew and grew
Into the names we have today,
(Names that are difficult to say).

Altostratus, cumulus,
Stratus fractus, nebulosus,
Cirrostratus undulatus –
Cumulonibus capillatus!

Try!

But great white whales
And billowy sails
Are still there in the sky;
And castles, towers
And cauliflowers;
Giants, deep in sleep
And wandering sheep –
They're all still there,
High in the air.

Look up!

More poetry to enjoy by Hilda Offen

Blue Balloons and Rabbit Ears
Shortlisted for the CLiPPA Poetry Award

'An appealing collection for young children, illustrated by the poet. Full of fun and rhyme and rhythm and a variety of verse forms, it includes thoughtful themes about nature and history too.' – **CLiPPA judges**

'An enticing mix of original nursery rhymes and poems to entertain all ages.' – **Parents in Touch**

'The playful title perfectly captures the spirit of this delightful collection. Readily accessible through their strong adherence to rhythm and rhyme, the poems' subject matter will appeal to a wide age range ... a collection which children can return to for many years.' – **Carousel**

Message from the Moon

Selected for The Reading Agency 2017 Summer Reading Challenge

'Inviting poems celebrate the wonder, variety and possibility of a young child's world' – **Books for Keeps**

'There is a romp and a rhyme for everyone in this delicious mix of imaginative, thoughtful and funny poems' – **Lancashire Evening Post**

'Dazzling and inventive pieces'– **The Bookbag**

The Song of the Dodo

Hilda Offen is an award-winning children's book author and illustrator with many books in print. She won the Smarties Gold Award for her picture book *Nice Work, Little Wolf!* and her book *The Galloping Ghost* was shortlisted for the Roald Dahl Funny Book Prize. Troika Books publish her *Rita the Rescuer* stories as well as *Blue Balloons and Rabbit Ears* – shortlisted for the 2015 CLiPPA (CLPE Poetry Prize) and her second collection *Message from the Moon* was selected for The Reading Agency's 2017 Summer Reading Challenge. Hilda lives in Brighton. She is a regular visitor to schools and libraries where her author sessions are very popular.